COVEN

For Marlene
Your spirit is deeply inspiring to me—
such strength, courage, heart & joy.
I am so blessed to know you. With love
always,
Sam

COVEN

Susan Deborah King

Susan Deborah King
May 2006

FOLIO
BOOKWORKS
Minneapolis

Published by
Folio Bookworks
3241 Columbus Ave.
Minneapolis, MN 55407
USA
612-827-2552
www.folio-bookworks.com
liz@folio-bookworks.com

Cover art: Golden ring from Isopata (with permission from the Herakleion
Archaeological Museum in Herakleion, Crete).

Book design & layout: Liz Tufte, Folio Bookworks

Author photo: Linda Mack

The author wishes to thank the editors of the following publications in
which the following poems first appeared: Quilts, *Prairie Schooner*; Release,
Potter and Bowl, Joyce's Clouds, From the Stone House, Warrior on a
Mattress Pad, *Arts Magazine*; Indication from Esther, *Twenty Fifth Anniversary
Celebration Book for Our Bodies, Ourselves*.

ISBN: 0-9744986-1-0

Printed in the U.S.A.

To all the covens of which I've been blessed to be a part.

My deepest thanks for their love and influence on my life and growth:

Early On: Rhayma Blake, Kathryn Stulla Mackensen.

Scripps: Deirdre Taylor Johnson, Sally Schwager, Jolinda Osborne, Robert Hamerton-Kelly, Marjorie Downing, Ed and Skip Meury.

Union: Renita Sheesley Banks and Reed Banks, Linda Jane Clark and Ed Pease, Beverly and Bill Gaventa, Jo Calhoun, Susan Savell, Walter Wink, Phil Swander, Ann Ulanov, Beverly Harrison, Tom Hunter, Mary Louise and Willard Hunter, Phil Swander.

Four Springs: Luella Sibbald, Sheila Moon, Elizabeth Howes.

Afton/Nineveh: Sharon Hulburt, Doris White, Lola Merritt, Carol Delsole, Harriet Van Valkenburg, Helen Kane, Cornelia Whitson, Ellen Russ, Charles Decker, Linda Schmidt, Rebecca Elowyn, Dawn Sickler, Cheryl Sickler, Paul Tull, John and Demaris Hollembeak.

FIR: Rosalyn Chuvala, Eileen Harrington, Claire Willis, Paige Gillies, Lake Dziengel, Donna Calacone, Morgan Poldron, Leslie Goodale, Gale Sharpe, Marie Manthey, Jan Neville, Cindy Johnson, Jan and Charlie Lloyd.

Wood Thrush Poets: Polly Brody, Pit Pinegar, Patricia Fargnoli, Geri Radacsi, Jean Tupper, Carole Stasiowski, Patricia Ann Ryiz, Morgan Finn.

Connecticut: Patricia Finley, Ann Chapman, Chris Morrow, Charles Kinney, Kathy Callahan, Lynn and Colin Harrison, Harriet Kessinger, Scott and Betty Hill, Lisa and Bel Paulson, Ron and Sue Knape, Peggy and Ed Sanford, Cheryl and Dave Purvis, Nadine and Peter Oundjian, Mary Zeman, Peter Lyons, Jim Scrimgeour, Charlene and Dean Moll, Ann and Ab Spencer, Amy and Paul Schumacher, Debbie Rundlett, Amy Feucht, Cynthia Cuthbertson, Joyce McKenna, Brendan Galvin, Pearlyn Goodman-Herrick.

The Granny Pack: Renee Macomber, Anne Seltz, Anne Newhart, Marlene Slettehaugh, Martie Van Roekel, Yvonne Pearson, Nikki Lewis.

Mayflowers: Sara Stout, Elizabeth Shipton, Judy Lund, Cynthia Andrews, Jean Thomson, Lisa Reed, Barb Souther, Nancy Gores, Jinny Humphrey, Vivian Stuck.

Minneapolis: Susan Allen Toth, Pamela Hill Nettleton and Bill Schrickel, Julie Neraas, Joan Poritsky, Ann Manning, Sonia Cairns, Patricia Runkle, Penny and Bill George, Doug and Carol Baker, Dobby and Jane West, Nor Hall and Roger Hale, Jack and Ann Cole, Wilson and Gayle Graham Yates, Carolyn and Philip Brunelle, Dave and Ann Buran, Hazel Belvo, Marcia Cushmore, Lynn and Carol Truesdell, Norm Carpenter, Susan Marie Swanson, Jim and Susan Lenfestey, Carol Belz, Kathy Quick, Joan Byhre, Cindibeth Johnson, Pam Wynn, Martha Postlethwaite, Wendy Nilsson, Parker Trostel, Mim Hansen, Jan Mattox, Judy Takkunen, Lisa Taylor Lake, Jim Rogers, Ben and Lynn Oehler, Catherine Senne Wallace, Mike and Roseanne Monten, Dee Gaeddert and Jim Dorsey, Hal and Maggie Watson, Bruce and Carol Robbins, Leslie Sendon, Daphna Stromberg, Bob and Alice Strobel, Linda and Warren Mack, Susan Thornton and Paula Childers, Star Hausladen, Myra Starkenburg, Joan and Jack Parsons, Alice Schroeder, Karen and Scott Harder, MJ McGregor, Sheryl Scheller, the community of the ARC Retreat Center, and many members of Plymouth Congregational Church.

The Community of Cranberry Isles, Maine.

Special thanks to my husband, Jim Gertmenian, for his patience and support, and my daughters, Emily Gertmenian and Enid Gertmenian-King and to Liz Tufte for the inspiration of her life and her belief in this book.

COVEN (kŭv⁄ən, kō⁄vən) *n.* An assembly of 13 witches. [Perhaps from Middle English *covent,* assembly, convent. See CONVENT.]
—From *The American Heritage Dictionary,* Third Edition

WITCH *n* [derived fr. A.S. *wicce.* Allied to M.Du. *wicker,* 'a soothsayer.' . . . Cf. Norw *vikja,* (1) to turn aside, (2) to conjure away. . . . Thus *witch* perhaps = 'averter.'—*Skeat's*] : an Elemental Soothsayer; one who is in harmony with the rhythms of the universe: Wise Woman, Healer; one who exercises transformative powers: Shape-shifter; one who wields Labrys-like powers of aversion and attraction—averting disaster, warding off attacks of demons and Magnetizing Elemental Spiritual Forces. *Canny Comment:*

> The superior learning of witches was recognized in the widely extended belief of their ability to work miracles. The witch was in reality the profoundest thinker, the most advanced scientist of those ages.
> —Matilda Joslyn Gage
> — From *Wickedary* by Mary Daly

CONTENTS

COVEN

for WTP

They form a circle.
It's not what you think.
Into the center
they cry their truths.
There is no queen.
They form a circle.
Each is received.
Where did you get that idea?

Each one speaks.
They feed each other
sumptuous soups,
cakes with berries and cream,
and, together facing inward
their seated bodies make a vessel.
It's not what you think.

Into it they pour and pour
passions that cannot be killed
morose husbands, lovers on the run,
a challenged-to-the limits child,
enfeebled parents, the boss
they'd like to throttle, an ailing
beloved dog, losses, costs,
grief and fury over bombs and rapes,
the children, the children,
an herbal hotflash-easing mélange,
lavender lotion — one of them
gives a neck massage.

A second delights in hair earlier
adorned with a snowflake snood.
Another reports that on the way
to a certain out-of-the-way shop
having a sale on pleasuring tools,
her elastic snapped, dropping
down to ankles her drawers!
They let fly their colors:

they plot their moves
with hoots and swoons — shrieks.
Where did you get that idea?
It's not what you think.

They form a circle
and mix it all up, stir,
let it stew, brew, salt it
with tears, pepper it,
pepper it with laughs,
deep-bellied to high pitched.
It bubbles, seasoned with
their pricklings and differences,
envies, resentments —
absorbed, transformed,
simmering savory, flavorsome.
Is the drift of that idea shifting?

Out come the gifts — they're big
on birth, especially out of deaths,
from which they do not flinch:
a blown glass hummingbird,
a mauve mohair throw—
honoring the particular spirit of each.
From the elixir of one another's company,
they drink deep.
It braces them
for whatever they have to face.
A cone of power rises.
Not the kind you think.

It swirls into a widening spiral
that, as it picks up speed,
could sweep you into it,
sweep you into it!
They form a circle.

EVE

Spitting from her mouth the withered apple seed
she was afraid would be her last natural act.
Oh shit! she cried. Now it's the dainty-lady-
slip-it-discreetly-though-the-lips-into-a-
hankie-with-a -hand-tatted-edge- routine.
Oh! How I've loved to spit! To fling something
I don't like right away from me and not
swallow it just to be polite. And bleah!
This one was mealy, but I was warned what I'd
get for wanting to know how apples got here
in the first place, how they were designed and why.
How they *taste* for God's sake. For God's sake.
Yeah, that's why we have to pussy foot and cover
up, just because I decided to use my own mind,
to find out for myself. And what did I find?
This fruit could sure use some improvement.
From a ways off it looked so scrumptious,
so shiny, frosty, red burnished gold.
Pretty tempting, I admit it; I was hooked.
But what a let down! No wonder He was so
defensive and didn't want me to touch it.
Not such hot stuff after all. Hey. You know what?
I think I've just been let out of jail!
All that time conniving to get what he tried to
keep away. Fine! I'm out of here. Done me a favor.
I'll just grub along and learn as I go,
test every clod to see if it's fertile.
Why let anyone else determine bad or good.
And if I'm not refined enough,
tough bounce! I'll wear my grubbing like glad rags.

Spitting from His mouth the withered apple seed,
He'd had no idea it would sprout.

JOLINDA

takes a chair and places it before the window
looking out over the ocean, the Pacific,
the largest body of water in the world.
She sits in an attitude of wonder, leaning
slightly forward, attentive, as if before
an altar or an oracle that will tell her
what is next or what her real purpose is.
And she hears it in the opening and
closing of the water, its ferocious,
unending roar; she sees it in
the perpetual reformation of clouds,
mists drifting and showering like
a gypsy's beaded curtain.
What would emerge if it parted?
All her strivings for love, for marriage,
for children, vocation and success
have broken, as these waves have,
five and six tiers of them at a time,
against these rocks, pounding and polishing,
wearing her down, diminishing her
until she is nothing but a tiny bit,
a slick, bright nugget swooped out and out
and back, out and back. Ashore at last,
set in the sand, she is dense and concentrated
as the golden agate she treasures now
between her fingers and thumb.
It is early yet and overcast.
She is alert and still.
A gull yelps its concatenation of laments.
It has not been daylight until this moment.

FROM THE STONE HOUSE

for Renita Sheesley Banks

Mornings then and there in the brass bed
under rainbow panes, your grandmother's
stitchwork Klee, my eyes opened to
a quilted lid coming down on me.
I'd listen for my heart — still silent as
stone. You'd been live for hours to
the cardinal, warblers, the indigo bunting.
Look, look, you'd say, *over there on that
wire, so blue, such a deep blue.* And the songs
you'd hear: *"Where Are You?" "How
Will I Go On?" "Here I Am!" "Four New
Eggs."* Though spores from mould on the
stones clogged your lungs, you'd pump
the old organ downstairs till it would
sound and then let your own versions
rush from you free as waters of the Juniata
swelling with snow melt. You took me down
to one of its creeks and showed me violets,
their petal chambers, purple tremolos
in breeze gentling the damp shade.

BIRD IN A BOX

It's a bright, mustard yellow box,
wooden, with plenty of vents.
The bird batters around inside
bruising her head against the lid.
She tries to peck through the sides,
For long periods, she pulls into
brood position: it's not such
a bad box; she's lucky to have it.
In light that cuts through like
magician's blades, she preens
her flame blue-purple quills.

BLOODY MARY

It's nearing Halloween.
I'm with two little girls
who inform me there's a story
they HAVE to tell. It's about
"Blutee Maree," of course. What else?
For two full days, wherever we are,
they go at it with markers and pens.
On the floor of the store,
in front of the headlines:
NO WOMEN PRIESTS!
SERBIAN SOLDIER RAPE TO BUILD
MORALE,
in the car past trees dismembered
and bulldozed for a mall, or
back at the house, obsessed,
relentless, they conspire
with whispers and squeals,
furrowed brows.

She was killed by a psycho,
they tell me. Why did he kill her?
I ask. *Because he was a psycho,*
they say, *a psycho-drunk,*
who didn't like girls.
She's dead and she can't rest.
She's mad. Better watch out!
They laugh. *She'll grab you.*
She'll pour blood on your head.
She won't stop till her blood runs out.
And she's got a lot of it.
She didn't want to die.
She wanted to be alive.
With glee they stab their paper
with red to show blood
fountaining off her like sweat.
I ask where they get this
almost ferocious gaiety.
From the air, they say, *from the air!*

HMONG GIRL

I have my life,
she answered instantly
when asked in what ways
she might be rich.
Oh! And my family and my friends!
My heart works.
My brain lights up.
I can dance.
She slides across the floor
in her every week pink sweatshirt
and black pants, landing
in giggles on her bottom,
this girl whose parents fled
when soldiers torched their
thatched-roof mountain homes
in Laos, who hid in the forest
grubbing for food and crossed
the Mekong at night under fire
in innertubes sucked under
by treacherous currents.
Her family, 8 sisters, 3 brothers,
waited ten years in a Thailand camp,
death walking every night by their beds,
for five rooms in an East St. Paul duplex,
for hot 13-hour days picking cucumbers
for an illegal pittance.
They could still sell her
soon into marriage. At nine,
she's a prize, already deft
at embroidering her family's story,
at stitching bright *pa' ndau* designs:
the elephant's foot, the snail,
life as an ever-widening circle.
After a beat of beatific silence,
a smile spreads across the smooth,
golden, full moon face of this girl,
who prefers her American name, Liz.
Two emphatic nods of her head.
Yes. I have my life, she says again.

LOUISE

She came on Tuesdays to iron,
the only day I rushed home from school.
She set up the board in the glassed-in porch.
I'd run in and bury my head
in the skirt of her starchy gray uniform,
then sit, just sit and sit, looking up
at her beautiful, full-bodied form,
her strong, smooth black arm expertly
shimmying the iron.
She'd take from the big basket, one of
many damp, rolled up shirts,
snap it open and lay it
back first on the board,
shaking extra water over it
from a Coke bottle
with a sprinkler corked in its mouth.
She pushed the iron back and forth.
The steam rose. She hummed. For awhile
I felt safe and warm.
She'd pause, catch her breath,
keep on. She took her time,
took pride in getting it all done "nice."
There were stacks of crisp handkerchiefs,
pillow cases, perfectly creased that smelled
like a meadow of clover.
I never knew where she lived or
what her last name was.
She said she had a little girl my age.
Every week I asked when
I could play with her
but never got an answer
from her *or* my mother.
I wanted just once
to go to *her* house.
Couldn't I at least
visit?

SMALL TOWN
GIRLS' BASKETBALL

for the Weston team

Even though their uniforms are cheap and porous,
   not silky and shiny like the boys'
Even though the bleachers are only one-tenth full,
   mostly with players' mothers,
Though no one has to pay admission and there aren't
   any hot dogs, Coke or candy for sale in the lobby,
Aren't any cheerleaders or players' names and numbers
   proudly displayed, alongside the boys'
   by the school gym clock,
Even though no banners are hung in the hallways
   wishing them luck at the state tournament,

They rebound and pound down court for a lay-up.
They dribble and pass, pass and pivot and
   hurtle themselves to the floor for a save,
     shouting out plays like hog callers, "Missouri!"
       Point guards up top, wings to the side,
       Center penetrates into paint for a drive.
They shadow, they dodge, they steal, they lour,
they wave. They go into "zone."
Snarling, they swear at unfair refs,
   their pony tails switching and whipping around.
"Lady" Trojans? More like ferocious Trojan *women,*
   avenging themselves at last against Greeks
   who took them as spoils and
   hurled their infants against rocks.

High five, low five to teammates making free shots.
Hugs and claps when a scrapper fouls out.
Protests when the coach benches an inept
   senior too much.
They work together as women always have and do,
   their own best boosters, cheering each basket
   with a "Sweet Sister!" with a "Get *Out!*"
   winning in this whether anyone's watching or not.
But, bonded, they shoot that ball

as if it were the world
as if by swishing it, slam-dunking it
through that sacred hoop they could
get "in a zone" where it would
change for good.
Then, the stands would fill with a whooping,
on-their-feet crowd applauding
the glad eruption on these courts
of raw female energy, of athletic excellence
too long held down.

WARRIOR ON A MATTRESS PAD

for Chris Morrow after her painting

Your mother smacked your hand,
"Don't touch those soldiers!
They belong to your brother."
Even though he had
invaded your room
to use your stripped bed
as a field. Let him play.
He needs to learn to take,
you to give. Stand back —
out of his way. Make a space
for him to do maneuvers in,
where he can manipulate
the forces of his fate,
a space you will later be
too abashed to claim
because you couldn't
get your hands . . .
could not examine this figure
inert on a plastic island,
its stance, its grimace, the weapon,
could not place it, turn it, move it
to act your plans.
Your muscles do not know,
cannot hold the posture of attack,
so your canvas throbs with red,
nothing but red, all shades,
figure and ground,
especially intense in
folds of the uniform,
diamond stitching on the pad
because you were forbidden
even to learn
how to fight
for breath,
a place to stand,
to dab and slap.
Nevertheless, somehow

you've managed
to plant your tattered flag
in this ground, a studio
where you've painted yourself
into the outfit. Yet —
knowing the fire you'd face,
you're still afraid
to take this bloody icon out
and show it,
own it.

JEZEBEL SAUCE FOR MEATS

for Kathy Callahan and her
Great Aunt Dean

As they mix the ingredients, sharp and sweet,
Grandma, who was Jezebel?
She was a brazen hussy, darlin' and she was a queen.
What's a brazen hussy, Grandma?
I guess that would be a woman who's not scared to stand up to men.
What men did she stand up to?
as they blend the mustard, the horseradish
the apple jelly, the pineapple jam.
It was really just one man, sugar. Elijah was his name.
Isn't he a Bible man?
Yes, he is.
They mix and mix for the sizzling Easter ham.
What happened, Gram?
Well, Jezebel, she worshipped a lady God, groves of trees and such,
and the Bible God, he didn't like that. He didn't like people
worshipping any god but Him. And Elijah, he put on airs like he
could talk for God, and he scolded old Jez. But she
put a curse on him and (chuckling and shaking her head)
he surely did shake in his boots.
What happened then?
Well, (sotto voce) *honey child, they ground her down to dust.*
But never you mind that. Just take some of this here sauce
with your meals, baby girl — it's like a tonic — as often as you can.

RETRIBUTION

Snuff films cast a light on the rest of pornography that
shows it for what it is: that it's about the annihilation
of women, the destruction of women, the murder and
killing of women — in which murder and killing are
just the end point that all the rest of pornography is a
movement toward.
— Catherine McKinnon

He (Jehu) said, "Throw her down." So they threw her
down; and some of her blood spattered on the wall and
on the horses and they trampled on her...when they went
to bury her, they found no more of her than the skull
and the feet and palms of her hands . . . He said, "This
is the word of the Lord, which he spoke through His
servant Elijah the Tishbite, 'In the territory of Jezreel,
the dogs shall eat the flesh of Jezebel, and the corpse of
Jezebel shall be as dung upon the face of the field . . . so
that no one can say, This is Jezebel'"
— II Kings 9:33–37

When they cannot control her movements
any other way, when they see they cannot
achieve her sinuous sway that imitates
snakes and waves and trees in wind, see that
they cannot make seeds bloom by themselves —
though their myths tell them they can — when
they cannot divine what she accomplishes
in the mysterious recesses of her sanctum,
they jump her. They throw her down,
stab her with themselves and trample
her until she is crushed, until she is
bone meal, until no one can say she
once was. It's the ultimate rush to
make her stop squirming. Then they
bathe in her blood, as they would
in that of any enemy, the substance
from which they once recoiled and called
anathema. Slathered with it, they

swagger and gloat over the spoils,
parading their prowess.

They cannot tolerate the dance:
synchrony, syncopation, fluidity,
fugue of movements — giving over
the stage for solos. So anxious when
not the only ones in spotlight,
they can't rest until all threats
have been struck down.

The earth has had all it can swallow.
Its unexerted power is aroused.
The meal of her ground-down corpse
has, at last, reached critical mass,
fertilizing the ground so that
mutant plants rise up thick and
tall and wild in a green rage
the "they" can't make their way through.
They bog down. Their machetes
bounce off stems. They're
overwhelmed, trapped in the lush
tangle, held by it until they
quit the struggle, enfolded for
as long as it takes them to metamorphose.

QUEEN

Tarted up,
all come on and strut.
Boobs bulging,
hips flipping,
sequins LA-basin glitzy,
jewels big, blinding,
bogus as sex role rules.
Pinky blond curls,
flossy, bouffant
flounces bouncing
skirt, slit, sloughable
as the skin of an asp.
Gams greased and gartered,
netted, silked.
Heels high as the clientele.
Lashes batting,
red-as-the-devil
lips and long nails.
No woman would dare —
unless loaded, way gutsy
or so desperate she'd be
called an out-and-out slut—
go this far femish
with this much pluck.
Before she floated
the boa over her shoulders
she'd be nailed
or snuffed.
But SHE can pull it off:
SHE's got a black jack dangling
and muscles with punch.

THREE LITTLE MAIDS...

Three red girls in purple pain
try to escape across the waves.
One carries a bag. They have no feet.
Where will they stay?
What do they flee? Why do they cry?
Let them be fleet. Let them be fleet!
Is there no place they can be safe?
Their tears fly to the skies.

On the streets of chance
three women dance.
Their hearts rising are purple suns.
Linked in a line, fiery, spry,
covered with blood,
grungy from scrubbing,
they will be fine. They will be fine.
They stride. They glide.

from monoprints

WHEN I WENT DOWN TO HARLEM

Sunday mornings
from Morningside Heights,
from the stone courts
of the seminary, where
I sought the white wisp
that was God with locked
hands and a hung head
and the liturgy stoppered
my roiling deeps, turbid
with trouble and pain,
I went down off that hill,
down 125th Street
cobbled with smashed glass,
bloodstains like those
on my family patio
smearing the sidewalk,
I passed chicken shops
roasting the only available gold,
a beat you could move to blasting,
passed corner gentlemen
rumpled and swaying
who, for my pale skin
and long, middle-parted hair,
called me Mona Lisa,
tipped me their hats,
passed vendors setting up
dashikis, setting up the faces
of Malcolm X and Dr. King
fluorescent on black velvet.
I went down Lenox,
up 128th, my face a speck
against all that black
and climbed steps of a church
that won hope like flecks of
obsidian from lava
and once inside wailed
finally with others
sobs choked back
behind walls on the hill.

I wailed my father, dead
from rising too high
and falling too hard.
I wailed my brother, who,
blaming my mother,
knifed her,
and knifed himself.
I wailed my own urge
to hurtle down and shatter.
Here at last I could unstop
myself. Knowing
what it was to lose all
to have nothing,
they didn't bolt,
they didn't recoil.
It felt like a home.
We whooped and danced
and sang until the pits
inside us rose up into hills,
then went downstairs for
collards and chicken backs.
Elbow to elbow at the table,
I could feel my blood beat with theirs,
my strength, a rock polished
by the sieges laid to it,
my skin wanting to blacken.
One big woman folded me to her,
called me her child,
but said sooner or later
I'd have to go back
to my own folks.
So eventually I dragged
back up the hill
sentenced to the father's
dry theologies
and my clean silent cell
where the broad, black breasts of God
were stoned and barred.

LO, HOW A ROSE

for Deirdre Elinor Taylor Johnson

"It came a floweret bright
Amid the cold of winter
When half-spent was the night."

We were in your parents' living room
where your father's plastering prowess
had trowelled the ceiling into clouds,
and we could hear the Christmas roast
crackling fat for the Yorkshire pudding,
when you played it for me, roommate
you'd taken home from college,
and you sang, out of the Episcopal hymnal,
out of your soul's well
into the darkness of my father
bankrupt and on a bender,
my mother sunk in a drunken fog,
brother in a psych ward, and me
trapped under the avalanche of it all.
Your notes told of how
it could come in the coldest cold
and petals of my clenched heart
broke into a floweret of light.
I put my nose to it to
inhale the hope, to marvel
at the beauty of its opening and
embraced you, whose
unself-conscious love was
strong enough to bear me a savior:
this heart-rose-night-light
bright twenty years now
for guiding me out from under.

HELP FROM THE MOON

for Claire Willis

Tonight, in your car,
you tell me that
your mother's back pain
is another tumor,
gripping and splitting her bone.
Now there are more than
doctors can count
and a cry for you
escapes her tough,
self-sufficient frame.

You go down.
Make meals,
up and downstairs,
laundry and bed changes,
kisses, tears,
her hands to your face,
"My little girl . . ."
"She loved me hard,"
you say, enough
so you can be
the "big people" now.

As we ride, you point out
the moon, white against the black
as bulbs you've just tucked
into the ground,
its brightness so magnified
by its cloudy winding cloth
we hardly need headlights.

It helps to look up.
The night is bruised
with such a radiance
we can imagine rows of
luminous tulips guiding
her into the dark before us.

INDICATION FROM ESTHER

Many's the morning I've seen you
out my kitchen window having at it
with a pitchfork in the border
by the side of your house, ruthless
with weeds, encroaching sod —
anything that hinders the flower.
Then the mallow sighs and
settles in. Under your care,
it thrives, nodding in wind,
soft green, pale pink affirmations.

No one I know knows better than you
how everything that grows has to
die back before it blooms again
from seed, bulb, corm or spore,
so if this impending death of yours
were anyone else's, I'd come to you
and beg for reassurance that your pain,
and mine at losing you, is
a seed coat splitting, that it's
all part of the order, and once
this breach is labored through,
dense, heavy, dark as soil,
you will emerge in an ether
intensified, bright as godetia's
burst-open hearts with petals
waving, Goodbye, I'm off
on a journey, or as was
so often your wont,
Come on over.

WHAT DO YOU DO

when your neighbor,
a tiny, wiry Yankee
with a gravelly lilt
and a twinkle, still
svelte in sleek gray
bob, gray flannel,
button down shirt and
a cardigan after six
kids — all grown —
she'll tell you about,
without boring you,
the youngest she wishes
would quit the stage
for something steadier,
though she helps him
all she can with
pin money she earns
clerking at a local
sweater outlet;
when she who's
always sending up
something for *your* kids:
creme eggs at Easter,
Santa ornaments
and thinks to ask
how's the little one's
eye problem, this
neighbor who will
always lend you
anything — from their
tall ladder every
Spring and Fall
for cleaning the gutters
to, once in awhile, an
ear when you're gloomy,
but who will only
very reluctantly ask
a favor herself (would
you *just this once,* while

they're gone for the day
let out the dog?). What
do you do after a doctor's
visit for a throat that
won't clear turns into
a sudden operation and
she's got tumors enough
down there to choke her
(yes, she smoked)
and you go over and
she, who's not at all
given to such nonsense,
bursts into tears
like a child?
She needs you now
and what can you do
but kneel by her bed,
put your own tear-
dampened cheek to hers
and notice for the first time
it's one of those wonderful
furry ones with a soft
mist of fine white hairs?
Nothing but this
could have brought you
so close, but
there must be
something more
you can do.
What is it?
What else?

AFGHAN FOR ROZ

At your crucial hour, I wasn't there,
so I made this to make up for it.
I had work of my own I had to take care of,
important stuff I can't now remember.

I made this to make up for it,
for not helping you load up the truck.
Important stuff — I can't remember now what —
kept me from at least bringing in dinner.

For not helping you load up the truck
you blasted me, "What in Christ's name
kept you from *at least* bringing in dinner?"
It was just too much that day. I was tired.

Another blast: "What in the name of God,
if not this, do friends do for each other?"
Sorry. It was too much that day. I was tired.
I hope these crocheted rows will cover my error.

What *do* friends do for each other?
I took pains: each row a new stitch, a new color
in hopes that this blanket would cover my error
like the rainbow, God's "never again" to Noah.

I took pains: each row a new stitch, a new color
to show how much I intend to be with you.
I want this rainbow to be my "never again," Roz, but
I'm holding back. The afghan is a stand-in.

I'm afraid love will swallow me whole.
I have work of my own to take care of.
Still holding back, I let the afghan be a stand-in.
Where will I be at your next crucial hour?

INFRARED WOMAN WITH
HAT OVER HER FACE

It is only safe like this
with a hat clapped over her radiance;
otherwise, she'd be arrested
for indecent display,
for burning them with it,
draw rapists or bullets,
or worse,
she'd terrify herself
with her own magnificence,
its unruly blaze.
An occasional shaft
escaping the brim
is all she can allow —
enough to give evidence.
But don't her arms get tired
holding it up,
its straw gaiety?
And how can she find her way?
She's blinded by it
and the danger is
that, thus confined,
her face will melt
in its own heat and
disfigure itself.
However, then there'd be
no threat. She could
remove the hat to
the top of her head
and freely expose
an unlighted countenance,
irreducible and undistinguished
as a cinder.

— *after a photograph by*
David Sokosh

ICON

I could not buy her.
It was the end of the trip,
drachmas running out,
and she did not come cheap.
She was painted and owned by
the man bent to his task
over whom she hung
burning at me,
following me around the shop
while I pretended there might be
something more captivating than she.
Bound in black, backed in battered gold,
her skin was of olive wood, color and grain,
dark as the fate of the Greeks.
Her eyes lined with the kohl
of suffering, of fury,
bore down on me:
I had chances she was not allowed,
could not take.
Her aspect was not unkind,
only searching and severe,
exerting the pressure of heat and wet
that swells a seed.
Why was I holding back?
Did I not know? I was alive!
Why didn't I spill riotous
as violet bougainvillea
over thick, white-washed walls?

IMBROS GORGE

Criti

We are going up into her
into earth where the Goddess
once reigned, the bare-breasted Goddess
whose realm relished the olive branch,
the bowl, the spiral and the bull,
where music, dance, art, play and making food
were the ways of the state,
where war was a foreign word
and her people listened
to the silent, earthen wisdom
                of the snake.
We are going up into her.
Our bodies together make the male
coming in to her shadowy domain,
where, to save themselves from extinction,
endemic species cling to her walls,
walls spattered with lichen pearly as sperm
down which weeping rivulets stream.
Golden drops dangle
from the edges over us
and a lone bird warbles
Her lost untranslatable Name.
We penetrate her narrows
and, pressing up into the crux,
we lie and love on Her bed
of pale, water-smoothed rock.
How much loving will it take
to reanimate her, to propagate
spirit enough to exalt, to exult
in Her estate? For this loving
deeper than this gorge in us
we will have to reach.

IN ANATOLIA,

this part of Turkey they call the "country of many mothers,"
there are seventeen layers of civilization.
The mothers are on the bottom.
They have been buried by centuries of progress:
The dancing virgin with upswept skirts.
The fat queen between two leopards giving birth.
The long skinny Madonna giving suck.
Twin goddesses skipping arm in arm.
Sibyls, heavy-bosomed, staunch.
Once they, bold and bare were the ones bowed to,
                                        held up.
Now they cover their heads,
scurry furtive behind doors men, from the outside,
                                        lock.
In Konya, in the Archaeological Museum,
open only upon request,
a clay face, millennia old, doleful, searching
peers up at me from Karahuyuk:
Please! For every one of us dug up
there are millions still underneath!
Is she laying their rescue at my feet?
I will stand tall and straight as one of these poplars.
I will send my roots through the layers — deep
and draw up their voices through my trunk
into the wind-rattled leaves,
and through the upsurge of sap,
their roaring chorus,
we'll be the ones redeemed.

for Sheryl Scheller

30

DESPERATION FLOWERS

You've kept it in for five years now,
how alone you feel in that little town
with three kids, work that drives throbbing rods
up your back and only pays rent on four cramped
rooms, Salvation Army castoffs, meat
twice a week, if you're lucky. Can't even
replace the pan with no handle. Always singeing
your fingers. You in your prime with night
flowers to give take in sewing, press
the needle up and down through midnight
while your buds tighten and yellow.
You tell yourself your eyes will be so blurred
from stitching, you won't see how dark it is
when you finally turn out the light.

Something — was it the landlord's refusal
(again!) to plug the leak? — made it all
come out. These troubles flung
like so many comets, white thorns
stuck in your indigo ceiling. The night
sky wounded to brilliance
by your cache of pain. You've put this
in a letter that reached me today.

I set it down and walk out back where
flowers I haven't been able to identify
are in bloom. Now I know what they are
through you. Phacelia. Deep cups cobalt
as Depression glass with white stars
shooting up from the bottom — what you'd find
if you peeled open choked down tears.

Bees are drawn to them more than to other flowers.

NEEDLEWOMEN

She possessed an art . . . to supply food for her thriving infant and herself. It was the art . . . almost the only one within a woman's grasp — of needlework. It might have been a mode of expressing and therefore soothing the passion of her life, the pleasure she derived from it incomprehensible to the other sex.

— *Nathaniel Hawthorne,* The Scarlet Letter

When relegated to the parlor or
forced to support themselves,
they contended with thread and material,
creating from their only recourse
Queendoms of linen arrayed with
rainbows of silk. If you think them,
bent to their sedentary task,
passive, frivolous, inconsequential,
consider the needle's point, its
sharpness, the stabs into fabric, how
they lanced their many grievances,
piercing through and through
the wooden hoop.
How they made of their confinement
garments, draperies, naperies
that would confirm in line and fit,
in color, intricacy, sumptuousness,
the magnificence of their own natures.
For what else, who else, beyond or
within their walls would do as much?

Yet were not the soft housings
they fashioned necessary as
the harder ones their brothers
wrought? Do mortise and tenon
require more skill, give more
pleasure than a French knot?
Girls of six became mistresses of
stitch: learned their letters, numbers
cross by cross, scrolled epigrams,
poems, made their names in chain,
immortalized themselves;

with satins they plumped a
robin's breast, petals of the
asphodel; with stems, the
fountaining leaves of willows.
Samplers were encyclopedias,
their makers double scholars.
They embroidered myth and history
on their hearts. Thread tributes
afforded long acquaintance with
Aurora, George Washington, Betsy Ross
or Minerva, leading girls to
the temple of knowledge.

Unthwarted by men's scrutiny or
interest, enclaves huddled,
where they ripped out Old World
patterns for open work, each
detail free and different:
no flower's shape or shade
exactly like another's.
Abandoning absolute symmetry,
loosening borders
presaged revolt.
Before suffrage, they registered
with gussets and darts.
Crafting and chatting
seamed them into a power.

By dim winter fires they flashed
tiny, silver wands and
on pillow slip hems, vines
twined and bloomed, on snowy
lawn, even rows of smocking
cropped up. Pale triumphs?
Their work, its vibrance,
voluptuousness pokes holes in that,
attesting to savage passions
soothed into beauty, into use by
sharps and chenilles, their
rhythmic, regular thrusts.

QUILTS

Women take scraps and piece together forms.
Dark diamonds of rag make Bethlehem's star.
As bits cohere, art keeps them warm.

While scraping plates or sweeping floors corms
of design come to mind like jockeying sheets and spars.
Women take scraps and piece together forms.

School calico ripped on a fence, Grandma's swiss worn
with Yardley's to church, Mother's robe dotted with jars:
as bits cohere, art keeps them warm.

Stitching alone or around a frame they laugh and mourn:
a salt for sugar cake, the snake-like mastectomy scar.
Women take scraps and piece together forms.

Darting Minnows of chintz. Birds in taffeta Flight, torn
twills a Drunkard's Path, Cabins in wool the color of tar:
as bits cohere, art keeps them warm.

They're what you do with what you're handed down, born
with or buy: trips that take you nearer or far.
Women take scraps and piece together forms,
as bits cohere, art keeps them warm.

SCARF

for Brita Been

She's woven it
a river, a river
of orange-purple
flame, burning
a hot streak
against my plain,
straight solid-color
brain. It's a color —
can I stand it? —
I didn't choose,
I'm not used to,
doesn't suit me
throbbing in my
closet strange
among all those
wintry shades.
It's checkered
down the center,
lozenges lane-
shifting along
the sides. At
the ends squares
squish into strips.
into stripes, diced.
Hopscotching
the whole length
are electric, ir-
regular, multi-
colored slubs:
fuchsia, cobalt,
citron, lime
like sunlight,
spectral, glinting
off swift currents,
like DNA, the
helixes, ongoing
entwined. Held

up to the light,
the colors, opposites,
almost blend.
There is only
the weave, threads
fine and close
as they can get
yet porous. Then
the fiery viscose
fringe at the ends.
I wind it several
times around my neck,
to swathe myself in
this warp to weft
joining of order and
the random, this
fabric paradox:
flodfarge, livfest,
river of color,
fire of life.

HECATE'S YARNS

I

A woman so ugly and so old, what could she
offer? A face riddled with moles,
her hands a gnarl of fingers. Her kitchen
is a cave. The only light comes from under
the pot. And who knows what's brewing there?
She leaves off stirring and shuffles
over to the wheel. You can hear her breathing
as if she pumped each breath herself.
From a basket she draws out the fleece,
sheared from the backside of all your
presentable features: the thoughtless slap,
the inhospitable phone voice, a coarse,
darkening stuff. Now there's a stammered sort of
humming — the agony of loss in a tune — as she
treadles into yarn all you want to be rid of.

II

In my December dream she appears behind a
rotting tree. In its cove Louise,
my neighbor, and I find yarns, deep blue
and purple, soft and ample for looping
into shawls to swaddle ourselves for winter.
I wonder why I'm with Louise.
She's so different from me — stays at home,
doesn't know how to drive — but
words from the old crone told me:
    Curl in and cover.
    Let the dark, the white cup you.

III

We each take our share
and spread them onto swifts.
We wind and they spin out
in planetary paths, or like hair
gone loose in wind.
They'll be what's died
and what must live, the balls
wound up in our pits: cries,
screams, the fists, the juddering
sighs, mumbled snips, spit
and everything else we let slip
under a sweet-faced grin.
We've got so much here
to work with. If only
we had the time.

IV

At the ends of meetings my colleagues hike
calendars out of back pockets, black
booklets chocked with "things to do."
In my Sierra Club version I linger
by tidal pools, sink down in flowering
tundra to slow the pace, ease the burden.
To have no time for ebbing, no still and silent
space to feel the knitting go on without an effort
of your own is a badge. Yet while strategies
are being hashed and schedules debated, we
can't keep our eyes from the afghan,
emerging in the corner from the needles and hands
of a laywoman like an emerald, blue, brown
stream from a hidden mountainside spring.

V

Because I took my colleague's standards for mine,
it seemed small that all I had
from a year of ministry to the black ladies
of St. Albans was knowing how
to hook yarn into patterns.
Every Tuesday morning the older ones
formed "The Golden Circle."
Several rounds initiated me into
the ancient curative ritual of Crochet:
Narcissa Wheeler, first in her family to college
and who, with bone china, silver certificates
and a chin lifted above chiffon ruffles
was gentle with my student's zeal,
  You've got to learn to work
  with your hands too, child.
Clara Knowles, after six children
stretched her husband's doorman's salary
to three heart attacks,
  Whenever anything tells on me
  I takes to my handiwork and pretty soon
  the knot inside me's all pulled out
  and I've got somethin' to show from my trouble.
Willette Judson, husband long since gone off,
her son in jail for dealing, got by slapping
down potatoes in the school cafeteria line,
  When somethin' don't make sense,
  like color you never tried before,
  draw it through and stitch it in.
  It could make a powerful fine
  accent in your piece.

VI

I thought of those ladies this winter
when I'd burned out, run down by
breakneck schedules, played out
by scripts written in the hand of
this age. I could not go on,
at that speed, in those ways,
those ever-giving, ever-smiling,
all-capable ways. I quit, fallow
as a field of brittle, snow-choked
weeds and dark inside as when the moon
turns away to face the night. I curled up
tight and mute as seed dropped down
and down in a cradle of darkness,
crying, What good this time so still
and barren, this place so silent,
so alone! The air around me packed
dense for weeks as dirt began
to move and slowly wool rocked
out of me. The balls unrolled
like petals, like flames, all that wound-up
rage and pain, waves and waves
of hues and heathers. And my hands
almost of themselves took up
the strands, to make something of them,
real places to wrap in, lie under,
spread upon and wear, gifts
unwinding from the mouth of death.

SKINK

I like the word.
I'd like to wear it
and slip sleekly,
swiftly, in spurts,
like to
scamper over
underherbage,
follow vines
to their sources
and, on stubby legs,
each with three
long, lovely toes,
climb stems, trunks,
to look at them close.
I'd dart over dirt,
crawl through juicy
leaf layers
munching bugs,
then burrow into duff
for a snooze.
I'd streak by weasels,
streamlined in my
bright yellow
racing stripes,
whip/whap,
ask how they like
my longer-than-my-body-is
bright blue tail.
Anybody snatches it,
I detach, scram
leave them holding
only
wiggle waggle.
Presto!
It grows back
and I just
flick out
stick out and
stick out
my forky tongue.

IMPERIA

Hafen Konstanz, Germany

She holds them up, pope and kaiser
rumpled, slumped, their thrones her palms
and turns them round to all degrees
to show how poor their power is,
how toy-like are the miter and the crown
compared with her breasts and hips magnificent,
the genius springing font-like from her brain.
They reign at her behest, though she could
just as easily drop them into the harbor's depths,
and, if they learned this truth, they'd laugh at first,
later be aggrieved, incensed — then, what rage!
Sooner betray the sacred than confess it,
they'd send their sorry armies out against her,
and go down, still groping for scepters, crosiers —
                                    wands.

IRON MAIDEN

What if all the women
once shut up in her
to suffocate and roast
with spikes driven through their
breasts, navels, wombs, throats
as she was closed upon them
by priests and magistrates
for being female, for having
and enacting desires,
for possessing powers,
opinions of their own,
what if they were to emerge,
centuries later now,
from this hideous chrysalis,
a shape forged from blame
to betray victims with
a sister form?
Some, tempted to revenge,
might descend en masse
on those who perpetrate
such torture today —
women are still savaged
by men who feel diminished
by our chthonic strength.
But most, healers, true
to their original call,
might enwrap with their wings
blindingly bright
the fear-hatched hate
and hold it like a cranky babe
in the sorcery of love, lullaby,
till it gave up to sleep.
But a few, restive still
with gargantuan grief
would flutter jittery above
declining ever to light
among brutes who would so
bloody the earth.

MADONNA AND CHILD

Tuol Sleng, Phnom Penh, Cambodia

Your eyes cannot believe
and neither can mine
that they would take you from your child
and rape you, that they would
make you watch as they beat your baby
lifeless,
that they would hang you
upside down and dunk your head
to near drowning in a pail of water,
clamp your hands and pull one by one,
the nails from your fingers,
and then, shouting at you
not to cry out, apply to your breasts
an electric prod
before
they slit your throat
flung your body on a pile
with hundreds of others
in the back of a truck
and dumped you into the pit they dug
and laughed, laughed
as they threw dirt in your face
to bury you.
And for what?
A system you couldn't comprehend
let alone assent to,
a thing not human.
Beautiful mother, I want to
I want to take you to my mutilated bosom
and run with you and your babe away
from those who numbered you 74
and took this gruesome photo.
I need a world-sized sheaf of joss sticks
to light a conflagration
that would release a monumental fragrance
to cover the stench of your death
and all the others.

I want to send up smoke enough
to irritate the eyes of heaven,
so a deluge of tears
will wash from our species
this heinous, unfathomable impulse.

THE GIRL ON LA CRUZ

There was one in particular the soldiers talked about that evening: a girl on La Cruz
whom they had raped many times during the course of the afternoon, and through it all,
while the other women of El Mozote had screamed and cried as if they had never had
a man, this girl had sung hymns, strange evangelical songs, and she had kept right on
singing, too, even after they had done what had to be done and shot her in the chest. She
had lain there on La Cruz with the blood flowing from her chest, and had kept on singing
— a bit weaker than before, but still singing. And the soldiers, stupefied, had watched
and pointed. Then they had grown tired of the game and shot her again, and she sang
still, and their wonder began to turn to fear — until finally they had unsheathed their
machetes and hacked through her neck, and at last the singing had stopped.

— "The Truth of El Mozote," Mark Danner

Every night for the rest of their lives
they will wake up gasping and sweating.
They'll feel her legs wrapped around them
like a clamp: Let go!
Madre de dios! Let me up!
They will grab their crotches.
Their penises will sizzle like fuses,
will melt like votives lit
for the souls of all they killed.
Ever since, on that very hill,
the Holy Mother crowned her with kisses
the day the petals of her sex first bloomed,
the love of God passed through her as
emollient song, anointing anyone in earshot.
To them it was a sticky, sickening sweetness
they tried to wash off with her blood.
But, again and again, she will come to them
in darkness and pour down the
devouring chasms of their hearing,
a wavery, weeping joy.
Do not fear, mis amigos! Behold
the glory round about you. Trust in God.
And all through the night until
daybreak, they will be counting
how many more heads they will have to
hack off to shut her up for good.

SHAME SHIFTING

a news item from central Turkey

Let me get this straight:
She was raped
and her brothers killed her
to redeem the family name,
besmirched because, for a moment,
she escaped to chase fiery wings
waving through clover.
Is that how it goes?
She was fifteen,
a piece of property to desecrate
and a neighbor, married, a father,
much older, took her down
as she crossed the field.
He had his way.
He pumped and ground
and spat on her when he was through.
There was a border dispute
and he showed those *bleeps* who ruled.
How is that again?
Her blood on her brothers' hands
makes it a wash, the neighbor's
got the upper no longer.
Her family's clean, relieved
of ruined goods,
the rapist scot free,
the murderers too,
and she, dark-eyed, spirited, nubile,
coming up as weeds.
Have I got it now?

FOR RHAYMA

oldest friend and true

When he came through the second floor window
of the house you earned the money for yourself,
stood over your bed, big, black, bug-eyed,
grabbed you by the neck,
struck blow after blow to your face,
drove a lifetime of terror
into your soft, coffee brown eyes,
when he choked you
until you were almost gone,
then shoved you down and growled,
Bitch, just give me your cash,
leaving you a broken jaw,
black and blue blotching your flawless olive,
you whose presence
ready and lambent
attended my deepest gloom,
I wanted to forget that he, no doubt,
was grappling with dooms of his own
and losing,
that he had no friend like you —
a tall candle lit to dissipate his darkness,
that a drug was likely his only refuge
from no job and an unheated
graffitied-over hole or
nothing but the pavement.
I wanted to blot all this
from my pacifist, colorblind mind
and beat him harder
than he beat you
for almost snuffing
the slow glow that shored up
my guttering life.

POSSE

in memoriam, RF

We could surround his house,
honored citizen responsible
for the town's new library shelves,
father who, every day
when she was a child
plugged with a snotty rag
our friend's mouth,
bound her arms and said,
Don't you dare
tell anyone of this,
or, see this pen knife.
The blade is sharp —
he opened it at her throat —
I'll cut you, these sorry
little tits of yours.
removed the rag and
ordered her, *Now, suck me off.*
He forced her too. He was big
and there was always blood.
Now we've found her
after her many, many tries
dead, red wristed,
the only love she understood.

We could surround his house
at nightfall and let our songs go up.
We'd start with lullabies
gentle and soft. The ones
she should have heard.
Go on with love songs
full of longing and sorrowing fire.
Then the blues, blue
as bruises concealed,
the last moment of dusk.
If he comes out and shouts,
What the hell is this? Knock it off!
we'll notch it up, lift the pitch

to shrieks and wails. We'll
keen like Irish mothers
when a child's been killed.
We'll kuln like Finnish cowmaids
who'll starve if their calls
aren't loud enough
to home the cow.
We'll spell each other
day and night, night and day,
replenishing our ranks,
and never
resort to force
until we bring him down,
until he crawls,
shamed to his bones,
to his marrow cells.

with thanks to Annabel Stehle

THERAPIST

for Patricia Finley

It wasn't what she said,
not her words that I remember,
nor her fine, divining mind,
for that she had.
It was more walking through a back gate
into her garden blue with irises
to the little house outback, that
she took this space, half
consulting room, half sculpting studio,
separate from her family, as hers.

Formless, in a heap of fear,
I waited in there to see her.
She always entered smiling.
It was more her hair, half
almost white, half black and
streaked with blacker black, with gray,
more the statue by the gate she'd
brought out of stone of Rima,
bird girl of the jungle,
standing in a bower of rhododendron,
palest pink, confident in her body,
breasts held forth full and bare.

It was that when the hurricane
felled her huge, magnificent oak,
her *axis mundi,* her shelter,
laying waste to beds and paths
she'd given years to mapping
and fashioning, she grieved
as if for a person dear
and started carving from its stump
whirling figures, a totem: lion,
griffin, sphinx, fool, soaring
Holy Spirit bird, a work
she never expected to finish.
It would be in process forever.

But it was most her goddess in marble,
chiseled from a precious, salvaged
chunk, gift of a peer, emerging
from the dragon's mouth whole
that healed my dream of a field
of scarcely breathing women,
myself among them, charred.
In it she held out her hand
and pulled me to my feet,
raw and bloodied, utterly exposed.
I grew new skin under her care
and learned that I could and how
to shape the hard, resistant
materials of disaster.

ZELIA'S REMEDY

When Zelia comes up against a block
that dams the flow of her life,
she wakes in the dead of night and
bathes in a trapezoid of moon milk
pooling on her floor. She sits
naked in the dark, rapt and
silent, her heart open and
empty as the Ark to
the Absence that begets Presence.
As long as she can stand it,
she waits, staring at
the block's blank face.
Rage builds up inside her.
She wants to stamp and
kick and faint.
She hollers at the stars,
curses each one of them,
spitting their names:
Sirus! Bettlegeuse!
How dare they flaunt their light!
How cruel for them to keep their distance,
to twinkle and blink,
unmoved by her plight.
What could draw them closer?
What could dislodge this stopper?
She stabs at the dark with
the fuschian blade of her pain,
assaults it with tears only
this much despair can unleash,
and gradually they wash away night's
india ink, exposing dawn's dewy roses
underneath that fade, finally,
into the blue of day.
The clot within her is dissolved
and she dons the cape she's sewn
with the threads of love running through
all trial and whirls and whirls
around the quickbeam, a dance of
thanks, a dance of life
beginning again to flow.

DIAMOND

for RC

Before chronic fatigue set in,
Sunday, day of rest, she'd plan to take in
a service, a class, a rehearsal,
lunch with someone, a five-mile hike,
a party, a meeting.
Now all she could manage was a stroll,
a very slow one,
a few paces into the woods near her home.
She could barely hold her head up,
exhausted from breakneck, high-gear years
of rising, against tremendous odds, to the top,
bettering her hard-knocks childhood,
kicking addictions
and being the sole support — because
her husband absconded when they were very young —
of three college-graduated children.
She could feel a delicate breeze
cool on cheeks hot with exertion.
Drawn to the broad, commanding trunk of
a Norway pine, she staggered over to it
and leaned her full weight, so much
lighter than just months before,
against its sturdiness.
She could feel its energy surge
and transfer to her.
Her pulse picked up.
Her head, her vision cleared.

At her feet she saw it.
Presented like a troth.
She judged at least a carat,
so much larger than the one
she'd grieved the loss of so long.
Had someone dropped it?
If so, how could it be returned?
It would be terrible to have something so
precious slip off unnoticed.

On the other hand, how much
might it be worth?
She could always use the money.
Debt was a tireless hound.
With effort, she bent down to pick it up.
Why, it was just a sap globule,
a jewel of congealed resin!
She'd found herself in a living fairy tale.
This was the prize and she'd gotten it.
If, in trying to keep from being eaten alive
by a witch or giant,
you used up all your wit and heart,
it would come. Something you'd had all along,
but couldn't see until you were
completely run down.
She knew now what it was,
that golden egg the goose laid every day.
It was the sun.

SUFFRAGETTES

A Gratitude

To you, who marched, hatted, in white muslined ranks
before us, "Votes for Women" sashed across your breasts;
who wore under-the-radar brooches
of color-coded jewels: peridot, pearl, amethyst –
green, white, violet for Give Women Votes;
who risked ridicule, revilement, violence
to redress millennia of oppression, injustice,
we give thanks for the rights we now have.
As girls we never heard what for suffrage
you suffered: destitution, force feeding, death
at the hands of threatened husbands,
never saw, though you led arguably
the republic's revolution most radical,
your pictures in our school books,
never knew the train trips it took
to speak all over the country, red shawled,
to often openly hostile groups,
the monumental pertinacity
to keep proposing the amendment
to scoffing, yawning, nail-filing senators
who tabled it year after year.
Our daughters will – *and* our sons.
And when we take up our ballots,
beneath the slate of candidates
from which we now have a right to choose
will be underwritten your names:
Susan, Elizabeth, Alice, Carrie, Frances . . .
For you, many of whom never got to do
what for us you made possible, and we now
take as our due, we will mark, press, punch or pull.

QUILT POWER

Are you tempted to think women of the 19th century disenfranchised, without influence, their works trivial, of no consequence? Consider the clout of their cloth.

Abolition Sweet Gum Logwood Copperas Chocolates   Log Cabin   North Star
Flying Geese The Railroad Appliqué (Dahoumey) Stripedy Cloth Homespun

Far more women than men were active − passionate in the anti-slavery movement
To unlatch then shelter the shackled, quilts were smuggled, sold, raffled, auctioned.

Benevolence White Work (stuffed and corded) Broderie Perse Medallions Bible Verse
Lilies Trees Everlasting Diamonds Cotton Cambric Cretonne Calamanco

Ladies Aid fancy work kept orphans fed and schooled, raised and steadied steeples,
though without a man's backing, no woman could legally be treasurer of her guild.

Temperance Woad Indigo Broken Dishes Brick Wall "Alcohol No Longer!"
Blue-and-Whites Crusade Signature Petition Silks Velvets Brocades Moire Satin

Women, who had limited rights to their own property or wages, organized for
Home Protection against battery, abuse, destitution, husbands drinking up assets.

Sanitation Madder Fustic Stars/Stripes Stars/Bars Streaks of Lightning Eagles
Path of Thorns Soldiers' "Comforts" Sheeting Sacking Osnaburgs   Worsteds

Through fairs and bazaars women's quilt sales raised more ("remarkably!" said
Lincoln) to relieve war suffering, establish hospitals than the whole U. S. Treasury.

Suffrage Turkey Red Cochineal Courthouse Steps Shoo Fly Schoolhouse
Sawtooth Bull's Eye Hourglass Daffodils Chintz Calico Palimpores Percale

Stitchery funded the decades-long drive, strongly opposed, to the 19th Amendment,
each scissoring severing bondage, each needling, ballots poked through for the vote.

Friendship/Betrothal Double Pinks Perkins Purple Albums Crazys Wedding
Rings Delectable Mountains Autograph Cross Fakes Exotics Scenics Florals

To warm westering women on their way to and *in* the lonely new land, patterns
from memories were made for them by the network they'd likely never see again.

Stars: Variable Touching Ohio Feathered Broken Blazing Sunburst Bethlehem

Why did we not learn from texts all our foresisters accomplished? We did not
know what covered our beds. What might be different if we had? Now that we *do*?

— *With thanks to Evelyn Beaulieu*

APRONS

Home:
clothing, growing, neatening, cleaning, feeding,
how did tending to these things become anathema,
the emblems of such toil untied
and thrown onto the rummage pile?
Get out the iron, that ancient artifact,
and smooth out the creases of neglect.
In them read our mothers – bound, yes,
to these patches of cloth, their only fields,
but keeping us alive, warm, nurtured, safe
themselves amused with the art
of blind hemming organza sashes,
edging and enriching with teneriffe
embroidering ginghams with distinctive
flourishes: ghostings, at least, for their names.
Think of them as blazons of nobility,
the female strain, proudly displayed
not on poles but worn over the loins, locus of our origins,
saying with all the craft that went into them:
this, where we come from, is a sacred precinct,
the Goddess's triangle. Without them,
domestic ceremony goes unhallowed,
our clothes get spattered and we've
forgotten how to get out the stains.
If we don't scrub or sort, simmer or sew,
the whole world almost our arena now,
without brooms, the replenishments, the protection
of hearthfires banked under our own roofs,
the rat race could run us into the ground.

with thanks to Dorothy Sauber

JOYCE'S CLOUDS

Days in her cubicle
doing the clerical
job that barely feeds
her family, she knows
they go by without her,
that right now they are
folding golden furrows
across the sky
she can't see from
this room without a window.
No one will pay her
to wait on a hillside,
focused and poised
for the instant
one of them draws itself
down over the valley
like the Temple's veil
or what escaped from
behind it when it was rent —
the holy mauve-pink
mist of the Presence,
and for X milliseconds
to expose her silvery,
gelatinous, light-sensitive
ground to it and let it
change her by leaving there
a lasting impression of Itself.
Since her husband
boozed his way out of the house,
there is no time
for the film, stretched
across her chamber's floor,
to seize the sword of light
that cuts down through
the storm's black boil;
no way to catch fugitive
spirit puffs
the river reflects and
crumples like tossed drafts

moving downstream with
the perpetual permutation of
dreamflow, inexorably
bound for the falls,
black water
pouring over the edge —
so many undeveloped rolls
unspooling in the sun,
spoiling themselves.

INCUBATION

It has been so long since
she allowed herself —
too pressed, too preoccupied —
to lie down in the abiton
the morning sun casts
through long, narrow windows
across her living room rug.
But today she relents;
fatigue and aching shoulders
have melted her guard.
Stretching and groaning
like the dog beside her,
she settles within the frame
of this container, dozes
and warms, blank inside
as the negative of a snow-
comfortered lawn. Blessed
indolence that lasts three
quarters of an eon, until
an ice chunk clattering
off the roof rouses her.
She hears murmuring in the
gutters and finds herself
a waking vine sprawled
over the trellissed light,
refreshed from a dream
of green tongues starred
with large purple flowers.

WILD GRAPES

for Patricia Fargnoli

You say you want to move from here
where widening the Interstate
has chawed your precious green
down to a narrow strip of
grass and bushes and maples,
that the wall they're hammering up
behind it is a joke against the
perpetual breakneck howl.
You want deep woods, a hermit thrush,
hyssop and hepatica, the only rush
that of a brook, far from its source
　　　　　　hurtling home.
But look! How they've wound their way up
through the remaining brush, up through
the filth and tangle into the trees!
How they dangle, heavy, profuse,
their lush purple deep as the sky's last light
over your head, within reach!
How the air is thick and sharp
　　　　　　with their pungence!
Pluck one from a cluster!
Squeeze the fruit from its skin into your mouth.
Spit out the pit and taste, late in your season,
compromised, but undaunted as these vines,
the tart sweetness of
being just where you are right now.

TURTLE ON RT. 302

Big as a boulder
with razor jaws and
a hooked, anguineous tail,
she lumbers across asphalt
rolling tank-like over the
curb through traffic which
slows or swerves to skirt her.
She lifts one clawed,
nub-ridden leg at a time:
right front, left back,
left front, right back,
slow as tectonic plates.
Natives called her
First Land, First World,
said her gracious back
rose from water
to support us because
we were too beautiful
to allow to drown.
She bears the knobby,
deep green tiles of her shell,
each one a miniature,
many-stepped temple
away from the eggs
she's tucked into lot sand,
toward the pond, its
slurried springs, as if
nothing we can do will stop her.

ZELIA LEARNS THAT HER HOMETOWN HAS BEEN DESIGNATED A NUCLEAR WASTE DUMP SITE

No! Not in these hills whose green
        in spring spreads like a blush
        over her whole body at a sudden,
        longed-for declaration of love.
        Not here, where they rise
        and fall along the river that
        runs through them like a birth canal,
        their soft mounds scarred so far
        only with the pieced patchwork of
        fields and farm houses, a few
        trailers at most.
        Why can't they put it somewhere else,
        a place already fouled?
        Why can't they dispose of the need
        for a site like this completely?

        This is home, where her mother
        in a bibbed calico apron lowers
        her braid-haloed head to
        take from the oven rolls
        whose aroma censes every corner
        and will feel light as clouds
        in her mouth, where gold is
        a fully-tasseled field, hay
        baled and stacked in the barn,
        and milk smelling of it filling
        the tank in the parlor under her
        father's hand, big, red and square enough
        to pull a tangled calf from its cow.

        She's not convinced by "safe as humanly possible."
        She remembers the funds raised to
        reinforce the church's basement,
        the tar that sealed it up and when,
        after rains, the river rose and
        concrete walls a foot and a half thick

soaked through like a sopping sponge —
how two miles from the water
sump pumps burned out and flooded.
And she's read that the stuff
they want to dump is already
eating through its present receptacles.

In her dreams ears blacken inside
their husks, her brother's bald
children vomit phosphorescent blood,
burn holes replace the faces
in her family album,
cows bawl until they drop,
and over it all a question
flaps like a baleful banner:
How did we come to defile
the place that gave us suck?
And she wakes raising her arms
to divine from the sky
enough tears to cleanse the earth.

DIANA'S TRIUMPH

after a photograph by David Sokosh
of Stanford White's "Diana"
in the Metropolitan Museum of Art

They may think they have me in a cage.
They may think they've
stopped my swiftness here in stone
so they can ogle these
perfect pomegranate breasts
they'll never put their hands upon,
but my arrow, notched and drawn,
will zoom through any bars
they can erect, will arc
right to its mark.
With these tips I've filed
sharp as the horns of a crescent moon
and poisoned with the milk of its light,
I aim to doom all enemies of the wild, all
tamers who disparage night's
long silvered shadows in favor of the sun,
those whose blood does not speed but
freezes at the howling of my hounds,
whose limbs stiffen against the dance,
the mountaintop revel under stars —
around fire, the circle of abandon.

I'm after hearts who denigrate
the raith and synergy of covens,
the purely female arts of aiding birth
and curing some with club moss, others
with gold or sulphur or sepia;
those who clean cut centuries-old Douglas firs,
home of the marbled murrelet's nest, to
build their own, who hack down
the civet's perch, burn the spongy refuse under it
that makes soil, and neaten it into pasture.
Because they are intent on kill and capture, on
control, because they are not content
to roam the undergrowth with me and notice
how ants, who feed on leaflet tips of
the acacia and nest in its thorns,
protect their host by patrolling against
insect pests and nipping at encroaching vines,
I will be merciless.

I will shoot until they surrender,
until they kneel before the wealth and
welter of my realm,
until they let it buzz and
curl and stink and scream,
until they marvel at its mess and majesty —
marvel, and that is all,
I will pierce them with my passion,
and if they harden against it,
they will fall and rot,
fodder for my hounds,
for dismissing
the power of my power.

FLOWERS ARE NOT ESSENTIAL ANYWAY

for B.

A miracle to her that blossoms came at all,
so, since hers grew so close beside the path,
and she was by nature such a generous plant,
she gave to all who passed, could not withhold.
Her blooms were vibrant, varied and profuse,
but because common, worth no particular note.
It was assumed supplying them was her duty
and their due. Her family and friends took rafts,
yet still complained: she could not produce
a certain shade, took too long to grow back.
"Cut and Come Again" her label read.
Presuming boundlessness, they cut her too far down.
No more bright scarves to pull from sleeves of her stem
for herself or anyone else. Dried up, rooted out.

INCANTATION

for N.

Today you've come apart in my arms,
your face red, swollen and gouged
by tears and I want, for your sake,
to conduct the current of words,
but no matter how I pronounce "light"
your darkness stares back at me
unblinking and flat.
I wish I could climb to that
aerie, high above the world
and find the word with
wings to break your downward
plunge, swooping under you
like a mother for her eaglet.
It could uncock the gun
you've aimed down your throat,
and more than that could
make you feel that if
you trust and trust to
the air and to that feathered
cushion under you
wanting your safety,
wanting your growth
that you would one day —
believe it! — develop
wings to fly alone
and grace the sky with
a rare and golden sailing.

LOST LIST: CLASS OF 1970

for SMS

With the 25th reunion info
came this list
I'm not surprised you're on.
Where are you?
Do I really want to know?

You were the queen
holding court every night
after supper in your dorm room.
We came to order
around your feet on the floor
and waited while you
flipped open your lighter,
monogrammed, stainless steel,
favoring, as if still wet,
your perfectly-filed,
clear-polished nails.
We ogled your complexion,
even without makeup,
burnished bronze,
your gleaming green eyes,
the shiny brunette bob
you achieved on those
impossible smooth rollers
that made us fumble.

None of us smoked, but
we were rapt before
your long, slim Kool, that
once lit, became
a scepter, a wand.
You dubbed me jester and
lip-synching Jim Morrison,
I slunk over chairs,
perched gamely on your dresser
leering "20th Century Fox."
Your laughs were food.

You lured us off campus
into motel rooms for
the first-time underage booze
I swore I'd never try —
my parents guzzled.
It made us puke. Not you.
Already the seasoned pro.

Stripped to the bra
that held your long,
mysteriously buoyant boobs,
you regaled us — virgins all —
with sex stories,
the pool of first-date semen
that ruined a mohair skirt,
your all-the-ways with Mike Trapp
that ended in the Mexican abortion.
Loyal subjects, we covered for you,
wrote fake sign-out slips,
fended off the dorm mom,
dispatched discreetly
the reams of bloody gauze
we unpacked from you.

The only time I ever saw your
hard edge soften was at
your sister's hasty, makeshift
wedding. Seeing Mike again,
best friend of the groom,
you shook. You crumbled in my arms.
Most of the 100 miles home,
we both sobbed.
Why did I care? By then,
I had a lover of my own,
whom you dismissed as
unsuitable — laughable,
and you your white knight
Air Force captain. For him,
you left school, left us,
abandoning a mind
that made incisive parallels

between the discovery of the atom
and cubism.

Over the war, at last,
our paths parted.
You couldn't see my protests,
my fasts, were aimed at
saving your husband
only that they spat on
his flight after transport flight
into the jungle.
Was it you or the Chivas
that banished me from
your dwindling retinue?

I was sad, but your spell on me
eventually loosened, though
several times a year,
you appear to me in dreams.
Captivating flash, who flew ahead
and tested dangers for us,
what dark shaft has swallowed
your enchanted song?

WOMAN WITHIN

I ignored her too long.
But she was silent.
I'd have had to bend way down
to see even her black ankles
and dilapidated shoes
under the door to the stall.
She kept her tears packed in
and private, even to herself
except once in a while there
in the public toilet
where no one would care
or ask what was the matter
if a cry escaped like steam
between the lid and the boiling pot.
Even if I'd have knocked
on the door and asked,
Is there anything I can do?
she'd probably have snapped
Go to hell! or more likely
not answered, choked.
But I forget that the view
I had of her was from above,
as if I were looking down
into the well of the soul.
Tall, worked to her bones,
arms tense at her sides, fists,
her teeth bared and clenched,
eyes squinched, neck muscles
taut as strained-to-fraying ropes.
How would she ever
get back her smile,
her willingness to serve,
the only way to keep her place?
How would she cope?
She'd be trapped,
confined, raging, until

unflinchingly I admitted
best efforts had failed.
It had not gone as I hoped.
Once free, though, she'd have to
wander. Without the old role,
she'd have nowhere to go.

PYTHIA

Delphi

They think they can understand
the language of the earth.
It is not even words.
There was a time they gleaned
the cursive of vine and leaf,
but they have forgotten vegetative speech.
They interpret sounds that come through me
into what they wish.
Yes, for a time their columns will rise,
their towers. They did not ask
how long or what would happen next.
As long as right now
they get to hold the reins
of the winning chariot,
go home with the laurel wreath,
to the shadow meanings of the oracle,
they'll turn deaf.
Earth needs rest: invent, invent,
nurture, sustain, produce, all
the giving forth –
she will sleep
until the accretions of their buildings and roads
make her itch.
The vapors I've been smelling
presage their cities
yellowed with smoke.
What a stench!
She'll writhe
and try to shake them off her back.
How they'll quake seeing all they've made
tumble and crack!
She will open wide to swallow them in.
This will not be the catastrophe they imagine.
In the hours I've spent on this stool

listening down into her depths
I feel how dark and soft
she is inside, how slick,
how like a lullaby
her mumbled rumblings
to one re-forming,
unborn as yet.

FRIEND

That day I watched the structure of my mind
give way under its stresses
and crumble on impact with the ground,
she came around the table to where I was sitting.
She gave me her broad, soft breast
to rest on. She laid her warm,
almost hot palm on the knot
at the nape of my neck.
No admonitions.
No palliatives.
No curses for the other parties involved.
She knew
she didn't have to say anything.
I took her other hand
and pressed it to my cheek,
wet with more tears than
I'd ever cried before in front of anyone.
It was quiet for awhile.

for RMP

SIBYL

Expect not felicitations.
Up against it, truth,
honed, hunched, lumpy,
she'll view you crosswise.

Her eye is soft.
She coughs, harrumphs,
will grip you in a vise of silence,
then dismiss you with books.

She smiles on pain,
all of it – ours –
recommends more
till you're torn – born.

Glory is nowhere.
What was it you came for?
Feasting on them,
she weeps over your dreams.

GOOSEBERRY JAM

for JB

Seeing her pile of clothes on the rocks,
on that remote spit of land
we'd have thought it was a suicide.
Why else swim out in such thick fog
to the little knob of an island that would
soon be accessible by foot at low tide,
the water cold as her husband's shoulder?
But it was the day before her last in
this summer colony and her only chance
to pluck berries that only grew out away
from the shore purpling among the thorns.

So she stripped and made for them
as if they were the last thing
left to her, the grail she'd sought
her whole life, worth the bone-rattling
shivers, cut feet and bleeding fingers.

It had been *anno horríbilis*, the crucible year:
her husband slamming away from
her chalcedony eyes, her skin flawless as
the Parian ware she's curator of
for someone less perfect, less refined.

She dumped the berries into a cauldron,
boiled them down with sugar into
a heaving magenta froth — a substitute
for the tears that came hard to her
roiling and roiling there: her daughter's
blaming silence, the totaled car,
termites, threat of a layoff, a tumor —
all of it distilling into a syrupy voilet liquor.
She poured it into bevelled jars, then
sealed them and set them on the sill.
Light filtering through them turned her
rented, inadequate kitchen into a chapel.

That last afternoon, she called those
who had borne with her in that place
and invited us to come. She had
prepared her table like an altar,
laying on it a hand-crocheted shawl,
wild sweet peas in juice glass vases.
There was rose hip tea and
scones, warm, light, plump
and the jam, a casket of jewels that
quivered as she passed it around.
True to her profession, she asked each of us
to say what object we possessed
most contained our essence,
something an archaeologist could read
to know who we were. When her turn came,
she lifted the almost empty jam jar.

SHARON'S COSMOS

Down the street that connected our houses
they would come,
bunched in her daughter's hands:
crepe wheels, red-violet outbursts
against the end of August.
This was before I could
notice flowers.

Her often folded arms, tight lips,
eye slits saying, I am *not*
an open person — never paid them
any mind again after
she sent out that first party of
blood-warm faces,
bright, wide
accepting me totally in.

TEA WITH WENDY

for WN

It's better than we imagined
even in our *mythic* England
to take these stairs up
from Keswick's cobbled streets
to the tea room,
oasis from the cares
under which we each labor.
Here, they have no sway.
We breathe, pause briefly
and give our full weight
to the plush rose velvet-covered seats.
We order things we can't find in America:
toasted tea cakes
studded with succulent currants,
smeared with their richer, tastier butter,
and sticky toffee pudding, a local specialty –
really a moist, warm melt-you-down date cake
with a pour of what they call *double* cream.
With smacks and happy groans
we savor the soothing flavors
feel the heat of tea, black
with a hint of bergamot,
going down us, October chill
vanishing from our cheeks.
We hardly speak, refreshed merely
by one another's presence,
the silent interchange.
Maybe we didn't expect to find
this much rest before the grave.

NOVEMBER ASTERS

for Betty Hill

Ninety, and she's driven over
to lay on my doorstep a bunch of
"Michaelmas daisies" that
have beaten the frost and
made it to Martinmas.
They come forth, she says, amused,
her eyes bright as stars of the first magnitude,
eight feet high and thick
after the trees are stripped
and everything else has faded —
a woman whose response to the coming dark
is burst after burst of gold
ringed with lavender rays.

RELEASE

for Linda J. Clark

I love this time of year, you say,
as wind plays the window
with branches, clicking
like nails of nimble fingers
over the keys of my bones.
Last leaves, fragile as
ashes float down
the graying afternoon.

At the kitchen table, your face
lusters like the apples
divulging their aroma
from the oven. Heat
bursts pungent juices from them.

When you play the organ,
music breaks loose from you
like leaves, firing their last
in a chill rip of wind. You
love this dying, this
driving down.

I wrap against it in your afghan.
I've had enough of crumbling! But
now you light a candle. This
blanket, the apples, your smile all
warm me till, finally, the tears roll.

You've known all along what
keen, sweet incense rises
from the breaking down.

POMEGRANATE

Mythic fruit, fecund
with rubaceous grains,
skin crimson as desire,
burnished as by fire,
what a stash you have.
What caves! Every
cranny crammed
with juicy jewels.
You bet, I'd break rules,
go for broke – banishment
to pluck your lobed globe,
luscious, plump and plumb
your grottoes and nooks,
cells where monkish seeds
dream of bulking up
buff with reddish pulp
soursweet, succulent, piquant
to burst on the tongue of God.
Yet, why should only He
enjoy your flavors, jealous
of your prolificity, keep
you gated like the many-nippled
goddess for Himself? No! Cast
naked outside the pale,
I'll taste you, let your liquor
drip off my chin and wrists,
bathe in it, stain my skin,
and wicked, *live*, witness,
initiate to a realm once
forbidding, once abominated
coloring up.

MIRTHLESS STONE

Demeter at Eleusis

With a daughter going down
and, with her, the vision
of going on, as you would wish
beyond you, carrying your traits
into ages ahead, it is here
you come to rest.
There is nothing funny about this,
or so you *think.*
It is not only her intent
but her destiny to be lost,
to obliterate her mother's influence,
to bathe in gloom, wash off
love's evidence, expose
the gleaming kernel of herself
until it swells and cracks.
Whether it sprouts a tendril
with push enough to surface,
to breathe green in the wind
can no longer be your business.
Your tears are not
the nurture she requires.
The world goes dark.
Your heart withers in its bony cage.
The town wraps you
in sympathetic embrace.
The ache persists, enduring it,
the only escape.
Don't you remember
how you rushed
toward that exotic element,
the purple chalice,
the horrid bridegroom
your instinct chose
to break you
to break you into bloom?

MOTHER/DAUGHTER, MOTHER/DAUGHTERS...

Early on I cast my colored lines on a page
to loop her, and moor my dinghy,
cupped like petitioning hands
to her piling, but she was a wraith post
and I fastened only on air.
I could not steal her eye from the pot
where she tried to stir a self
out of her own diffuse ingredients
stewing there. Having nothing else
to feed on, she consumed herself.
Nothing left for me.

My daughters want a place to form
their clay. I shoo them
from the space I use to build
myself with words, fearing
the mess their coming into being makes
will tumble my blocks.
I shout them down to the basement.
Their fists curl like aborted fetuses.
I notice how I'm most affectionate
with them at partings: when they
go to bed, go to school, or I leave
for the evening to trek up, up
the spiral stairs out of this
repeating pattern into a cornucopia
that will sustain us all.

BLUESTOCKING

They said my mother was one.
It wasn't till she died I learned,
when college friends wrote of her,
she'd rouse them all on a winter's night
and crunch off shovelled paths
declaiming poetry to the stars.
She'd smoke enthralled till dawn
invoking Quixote in his native tongue,
untwisting logarithmic mysteries,
parsing Latin clauses, but, by the time
I came along, she'd exchanged those
worsted blues for seamed silk hose,
girdles, then pantied nylon ones, and,
desperate to keep my father — though
it didn't work — played down her
magna cum, played dumb, got numb
on bourbon, bridge, quiz shows, soaps,
crime novels and hollandaise hand-stirred.
She'd put away Edna, Elinor, Eliot, E. A.
and the whole *Oxford Book of English Verse*,
along with that considerable instrument of her own.
She surmised there was no place safe
but loneliness to use a mind so whetted,
combined with small tits and too plain looks,
and that she wasn't certain she could endure.
Wits, zest, intellect brought more shame
than public nakedness, and, sure as spearpoints,
drove off suitors, drove off love. Among
rather too many boxes in her closet containing
hats and shoes she donned to model herself
soignée in brims trimmed with bright blowsy roses
or emerald satin pumps, I found the stockings,
electric blue to me, stashed, stuffed, rolled up.
Attracted to their color and their comfort
I determined to wear them, whatever the cost,
glad she hadn't completely thrown them out.

HERRING RUN

It's all against them: the tug out,
gradation of land, gulls, even this clouded
light, yet these alewives scramble up-
current every spring to preserve their very lives.
I watch them pitch themselves up over
the gates at Brewster, where I've come
to steep in salt marsh and fog-laced air
to wait for some exotic brew to
emanate from me: Darjeeling, comfrey,
or something new — a bayberry-spartina grass blend.
It's been dry leaves for some time now.

A fish leaps. We bond through our eyes. I know
the heft it takes to plod through bog,
squeeze up sluice and throw yourself
over the hurdles: so hard,
with children, job and a husband
to seize these moments of solitude.
But, locked in bone and muscle,
is the instinct for this jasper pond,
quiescent in a glade of sheltering maples,
a place to spawn, let eggs ooze out
and bide until, coaxed by some inchoate
pressure, they hatch teeming
ciphers that spell and spell:
"Now you can carry on."

MUSE

Curled in whorl of creme caramel tufts,
she snoozes by my side on an afghan
draped over the chaise longue.
Once in awhile she whiffles or
heaves a satisfied groan.
This is what she wants,
what she's begged, whined, yipped
and pawed for, stared me down
bright-eyed, wet-nosed and wagging.
I'm finally settled enough
to receive a clear signal,
pure silence into which
lines come, music, *les mots justes.*
But then, she lifts her head and cocks it
to apprehend what I cannot:
the inchoate, the ineffable
spurring me to listen further
to press beyond.
And if there's an interruption,
in a flash, she's up to
bark it down,
modelling alertness,
protecting my attention.
I stroke her. She licks my palm.

POTTER AND BOWL

for Peg Andre

> Our pots bear our spirits into the world.
> — M. C. Richards

Lean, medium height in an armless, cut-off sweatsuit,
she mixes, with an industrial-strength bread hook,
the dense, pliable material 600 pounds at a time,
then cures it in a vat for weeks or months or
maybe for generations in a pit, decomposed
rock, feldspar, silica: earth, flesh of spirit.

She cuts a slab of it with wire, slaps it on
a wedging board and takes it into her hands
to knead out the bubbles. It takes muscle to
get the molecules in clay to coalesce, to work in
the yeast of her own bacteria, to form a smooth,
round loaf that will rest for awhile under cover,
readying itself, anticipating form and contents.

The wheel has been turning from the start.
It has spun out galaxies and midges.
She puts her substance onto the speeding
bat, bearing down hard, pressing it into
a hive-like mass. The wheel hums. Matter,
seemingly inert, is buzzing like mad.

Centering, the dervish dance. Into the vortex
of the infinite, all disparate elements. Under
her star sapphire eyes all oppositions are resolved:
ancient racial hatreds, the open hand, the closed,
male and female. She squeezes it up, a phallus,
opens it and, through it, enters herself like a man.

She pulls up a wall, applying pressure
with her fingers inside and out: the dialectic
between destiny and will. She pulls it up again,
carving with a yellow plastic crescent she

got at a tag sale — horns of Ishtar, moon —
a deliberate hollow. The wall blooms, the
slightly-curving lip suggesting petals.

She slows the wheel, otherwise the rim will
fly off. She smoothes the surfaces with chamois
and trims it with scalpel-like tools.
The floor around the wheel is like a carpenter's
or barber's, clay shavings and locks.
A close-cropped blond, her hair has darkened with
sweat. Wiring it off the round, she dries it on a
board to "leather-hard" upside down,
enclosing a darkness. Sometimes at this stage,
the cat will nibble off interesting notches.

It's ready to be bisqued, the slow, lower
firing that makes it hard enough to hold.
She sets it down into a deep hexagonal top-
loading oven and tends it over days checking
the temp. This is Connecticut, but the room
it's in feels like the healing dryness of Arizona.
It incubates till it is fully baked and cooled.

From an ancient Chinese recipe, in a big, plastic
canister with a toilet brush, she mixes
water and minerals, including copper and rutile.
As if luxuriantly immersing herself, she
dips it into this creamy glaze. The second fire
should fuse it with the clay and transform
its pewter gray into a turquoise matte,
her color, the color of Changing Woman's touchstone.

She opens the vault-like door of the kiln
she made herself, a huge double-walled white brick
structure in an open outbuilding. Exactly what
the fire will do can never be controlled — what
design will range over the clay's surface, whether
the glaze will flake off like Eskimo pie chocolate.
Flames must just be surrendered to.

For one night, it warms in there with just the
pilot on. Gradually, she raises the heat to
over 2000. Constantly monitoring, with a
heavily-gloved hand, she unstops a peep hole.
Red-orange dragon tongues lick out. Inside,
they're lashing up around the pots. She
blows them back in to watch as, one by one,
very slowly, a row of cone indicators wilts.
Glittering high in the winter sky, the Pleiades.
All night long, she maintains inferno.

At dawn she shuts the gas jet off, closes
the chimney lid: two days to cool down, cocoon.
She keeps a record, logging temps every hour or so.
Too fast up or down could shatter everything.
Every firing's different. What has this one brought?

On the bowl the glaze has been fixed in
a state of flux. More, much more than she had hoped:
shifting tidelines, mountains thrust into misting clouds,
tilting wings, fluid profiles, all in the cool
green-blue of salt lagoons with undertones of gold.
On the bottom, spiral lines track its path evolving
beyond horizon. It has taken years to produce, eons,
this holy, glowing vessel offering up sustenance:
cereal, salad, soup, rice, a floated blossom.

HER *FOR SISYPHUS*

for Edna Andrade, after her drawing

If he had to have a rock,
if he had to roll it —
and he had, she had accepted that,
even embraced it —
it might as well be the one
she found on this homefelt shore
before she has to leave for good.
It looks like a giant's brain,
big as the globe itself, the size
of a whole life's struggle —
the tribute exacted for witnessing
what the gods are up to,
for copping to their perverse proclivities
and fingering Zeus.

The details — each crack and bump,
depressions, cusps, oases of smoothness,
every crenellation — show
she sees his ordeal,
must have known the drill herself.:
heaving it — the strains, the grunts,
muscles maxed to near collapse — almost
up and over only to
have it rumble derisively
                    back down.

What is accomplishment?
The sun, the moon rising,
falling as our chests with breath,
our heart beats' path,
the climb and slide
of our dramas, our fortunes,
and in sex the build up
of tension. Climax.
Denouement.
The mortal rhythms we were born to.

But to put a shoulder to them
grinds pride into grit,
into dirt, the earth, the ground
we'll be, we'll be under —
growth's only home. This gift
she's drawn from life for him
is hard, complicated, rough,
beautiful as Chinese scholars' stones
through which they engaged
in lifelong contemplations —
exertions equivalent — of the eternal,
the whole cosmological round.

BIRDER

for Polly Brody

Cardinals started it,
hailing her with
chirrups and chips
on her daily constitutionals.
They called and hopped.
She watched. They became
familiar. Before long
they were the *reason*
for her walks. Checking
eye to ear, ear to eye to
guidebook, "pishing"
to flush them into view
on branch tips, she met
juncos and crows,
woodpeckers and waxwings,
siskins, the ovenbird,
the thrush, framing them
in her "binnies," inscribing
their names in her life log.

She got so she could tell,
by its narrower, more
numerous tailbands —
even at a great height
when scores of them
soared over her Septembers —
the red-shouldered
from the broad-winged hawk,
and in the Spring
the slightly higher,
slower hems and haws,
the uncommon drawl
that sets the Philadelphia
vireo apart from its
red-eyed cousin.

At last she knew everyone
in her neighborhood, from
year-round titmice and
summering swallows to
warblers just passing through.
Whenever she dropped by
the Carolina wren's teakettle
whistled and towhees
urged her to stay, with
white-throated sparrows,
for a good gossip about
old Sam Peabody and
a drink of their brew.

She was moved by the rose
on the grosbeak's breast,
the fire at the Blackburnian
warbler's throat, the dark,
deep shades of the black-
throated blue, dropped
everything for a look
at a Lawrence's, sighted
in a nearby orchard, rare
as snow in June. So enamored
she pursued fulmars
to an Iceland cliff,
close enough to
see tiny water droplets
in their nares.

The lengths she'd go to!
Across six lanes to
pick up the electric pinking
of the prairie warbler
cutting through
interstate roar.
In Scotland, diving through
a bed of stinging nettles
for a corncrake. Up
the hot talus of an
Arizona butte, scared

and scraped for a face-
to-face with a spotted owl.
Tented nights threatened
with army ants and anacondas
in the Panamanian jungle
for a glimpse, which eluded her,
of the quetzal's
mystic blue green sheen.

And in East Africa,
over the savanah, the
flat-topped acacias
bee-eaters and sunbirds,
glowing like brightly colored
fruit, poured as if
from the sky's cornucopia
with sixteen new species of eagles.
At home when she thought of it,
that refuge she'd seen once
pure as if in the Pleistocene,
now overrun by mini-vans and
brigands hot for rhino tusks,
tears dripped into her dishwater.

A gyrfalcon, far from its Greenland
roost, swooped into her yard
in response. Just as she
buried a beloved cat, snowgeese
softened the sky with a nod
of their black-tipped wings,
drifting down a single white
feather that clung to her
coat cuff. And when her marriage
failed, and her arms in grief
reached up, a broad-tailed
hummingbird dipped over
to whir away her pain.
Like vision-questing Senecas,
she felt she had found her manitou.
But when it comes time for her
to go, friends will flock
and her spirit will lift over them
into a sky aquamarine as her eyes
plumed and stupendous
as a great blue heron.

EASTER WOMAN

for Pamela Hill Nettleton

I know spring has come in earnest
when Pam tucks her thick black
middle-of-the-back length curls
into a red baseball cap and
tugs at the bill; when she
dons her son's black and white checked
flannel, mud boots, garden gloves
and patrols her yard next door.
Though it will make her sneeze unceasingly,
she parts the hay mulched over
bulbs and other flowers so
spears of green can pierce through,
tendrils and tulip furls.
She marches briskly around the beds,
workpants legs swishing together
like hands when
a job is done well.
She means business.

Just as she's raised it out of herself,
out of her own dark ground,
she commands it to emerge,
all that color cold-shouldered,
frozen, held down.
No snow now dare singe
her tentative, air-testing shoots.
She'd no sooner countenance
anyone harming her own babies.
Once she appears, thus garbed,
resurrection is sure.

JAPANESE LAUREL IN SALLY'S GARDEN

It's bloomed in honor of your coming,
you say and yes, some of the pink-
white buds that look like star
candies have poofed into cups,
like the one in which my great
Aunt Florence might have offered
tea, a wheel of lemon floated in it
slowly spinning — Limoges, a kind of
starburst pattern from which to
sip a 10th summer. How many times,
a three hour drive away, I've wanted
to sit with you in this shaded
cloister you've shored up against
the nearby Mass. Ave. crowds.
Here, we're virgins again,
tittering over Joyce and that tall
black Irish professor in cowboy boots
we'd have said yes to as gladly as
Molly Bloom; back to when our
allegiance to each other seemed
more fast than that we now pledge
to our husbands — yours with his
job taking you now to Berkeley
and even less frequent visits. I
want your arms near as they were
when newborn twins coupled
with a full time job and I buckled;
and mine for you back from your
brother's self-dug grave and when
your first husband bludgeoned you.
When you speak — of anything — your
fierce passion makes me feel like
one of the women whose lights
your research and writing have
unbushelled or the bright gardens
your grandmother's paintbrush grew
on the china that glows in your
living room alcoves. I look into
your eyes, blue-green-gray as

a sky changing into rain and see
the time when this afternoon, with
maples dappling sun over us, will
seem far away as the one in
my aunt's parlor and the pale pink
skin, already creasing, drawn
petal-smooth over your high, high
cheekbones will crumple as these
blooms are about to. Yet the bush
exudes such a quiet, deep green aura,
almost as if it were softly breathing,
we both want to go over and embrace it.

for Sally Schwager

TRIPTYCH

What the Bird Goddess Showed Me

You can fly out of these patterns.
You know, don't you,
that you can? Here, let me
lend you a wing.
Climb on my back.
See how the wind
riffles like feathers your hair.
We'll swoop and soar
bank and dive, then just float
on hot bursts of air shooting up.
Nothing more marvelous,
just keep extending yourself.
What's that? You're quite
used to the groove you've worn
going round and round.
None of this sounds at all fun?
It does, but . . . But, *what*?
You can't. You just *can't*?

The Star

The flotilla of dreadnaughts,
an armada of black,
is closing in again,
but the target,
a bright, busting-with-color blast,
wavery rays shooting out from it
right off the map,
is too intense,
even with big guns, to overcome.
It just seems to swallow up the shells
like licorice bits.
So dazzling it is that, spellbound,
those menacing vessels hold back.
They want to quash it.
It poses a threat.
But in its parti-colored light

the ships look so dreary and grim,
so riveted with death,
they lose their bearings.
How did it get so big?
It had once been just a
purr of light you could
pick off in the dark
and flick with a little sizzle
into the sea. But it grew,
fuelled by opposition,
into an inexhaustible star.
Somewhere between them
a woman is singing,
sending up a vine of notes,
a seam to sew opposing forces together.

BEYOND

When women were asked
to explore through art
what the world might look like
beyond patriarchy,
they worked together,
and had a ball doing it.
There were few straight lines.
The shapes were wavy, fanciful, curved.
No ziggurats, pyramids, obelisks.
There were interlocking,
ripple-edged circles,
spirals wheeling galaxy free.
Much of it was uncentered, random,
amoebic: floral, aqueous, vegetal.
It looked natural, like the images
of space-time proposed
by relativity, like models
of quantum physics and string theory,
the way, as best we can know it,
reality, at its deepest and broadest,
appears to be.   ·

KNITTING CRAZE

The world is coming apart.
Ties with our allies are unraveling.
Moth-like holes have eaten through ozone.
Under rapid fire in far cities, with guns
in their arms, our children are shivering.
In our own, too many go cold, without homes.
Too much of our lives now are virtual, on screens.

Is it any wonder then that women,
the same who stormed the ramparts for equality
and younger ones who butt against glass ceilings,
have again taken up knitting?
That the yarn stores, like skeins
spinning on swifts, are swarming?

If our needles, enough of them, flew fast,
we could stitch it all back together.
With bright, soft scarves and sweaters,
with tangible love, we could wrap it
and warm it and cheer it.

Our world, dear, round and defenseless
as a baby's skull with its fontanel
we'd cradle and cover with a cap
of healing wool purled
by our own hands into being.

ZELIA'S DANCE

She dances along the edges of the night.
She laps its shore like waves of ultramarine
and faces out over its continent of ice,
black ice.
Her course is serpentine.
Her hips swivel. She lifts her arms.
Her scarving garments undulate around her frame.
Her dangling earrings tingle.
Her movements imitate the ocean's
constant flux.
She sings into the darkness
imploring it to declare itself,
to notice her, to partner her as an equal.
Her song floats out into the void like
slow-rolling clouds.
She unveils her breasts,
their incomparable roundness,
their lush handfuls, mouthfuls.
Her skirts part over her thighs,
yet
there is nothing but silence,
a jilting silence.
The stars, implacable, are unmoved.
She is alone.
But she continues, she continues,
she continues, she continues
winding like a vine
embroidering the edges
with her vibrance
until the sky at its rim
throbs
with colors it cannot swallow.

APSARAS

Angkor

Thousands of them dancing
round and round foundations
hold up the temple of the world.
Without their animation
the colonnades would drop.
The deity may preside
monumental in his shrine,
but under him, does he realize?
They, sea-foam born,
their sprightly forms
embodying mother waves,
on strong, supple-as-saplings
legs, shapely through transparent skirts,
their upcurved fingers, smiles,
mounds of the bellies and breasts,
navels, nipples, dimples, anklets,
the leaping flames, upgrowing plants
atop their heads
make the stones alive
and keep through horrors
wars, weathering, crumbling, time.
Maybe still, what we dream can live.

ABOUT THE AUTHOR

Susan Deborah King teaches writing and leads retreats on spirituality and creativity. Her last book was *Tabernacle: Poems of an Island.* She lives in Minneapolis and on an island in Maine with her husband, and is mother to grown twin daughters.

COLOPHON

This book was set in the Requiem typeface by Hoefler & Frere-Jones Type Foundry. Requiem was inspired by a set of inscriptional capitals in Ludovico Vicentino degli Arrighi's 1523 writing manual, *Il Modo de Temperare le Penne*.